To:

MW00878383

GETTING TO KNOW YOU
BEFORE I SAY
"I DO"

With love —

The Momma

GETTING TO KNOW YOU BEFORE I SAY "I DO"

DR. DARLENE TURNER

XULON PRESS

Xulon Press
2301 Lucien Way #415
Maitland, FL 32751
407.339.4217
www.xulonpress.com

© 2017 by Dr. Darlene Turner

All rights reserved solely by the author. The author
guarantees all contents are original and do not infringe upon
the legal rights of any other person or work. No part of this
book may be reproduced in any form without the permission
of the author. The views expressed in this book are not
necessarily those of the publisher.

Unless otherwise indicated, Scripture quotations taken from
the King James Version (KJV)–*public domain.*

Printed in the United States of America.

ISBN-13: 978-1-54561-553-9

To my Lord and Savior, Jesus Christ, thank you for your unconditional love!

To my husband, David, thank you for your love and support.

To my son, Dezell, my love, you inspire me.

To my father, Pastor Marvin Jenkins, my first fan, I owe you my success.

To my mother, Evangelist Estella Jenkins, I am a woman of God because of you.

To my siblings, David, Shelly, and Lirea, I will always love you.

To Pam, thank you for your friendship, love and support.

To my best friend and sister in Christ, Nicole, thank you for always encouraging me; I feel like I can fly when I am in your presence!

TABLE OF CONTENTS

PART THREE:
PRE-MARITAL LIFE

PART FOUR:
MARRIAGE FOUNDATION

INTRODUCTION

D o you know who you are? Do you know what you want in life? Do you know what you want for your future? I know this is hard to believe, but you may not know yourself as well as you think you do. Have you ever said, "I would never do that," only to realize you did exactly what you said you would not do? As Christians, we make our decisions based on God's teachings in the Bible. Ephesians 2:10 says, "For we are his workmanship, created in Christ Jesus unto good works, which God hath before ordained that we should walk in them."

God created us to perform the good works he put inside our hearts. These are the good works he wants to fulfill in our lives. Our lives are like road maps that lead us to our divine purpose, and our talents are clues to help us get there. Every plan in your life has a season, and no matter which season you're in, God has a plan for that season and for you.

People generally experience four different stages of life. Each stage is just one of the many good works God provides for us:

1. Living a single life
2. Dating someone special
3. Becoming engaged
4. Building a marriage foundation

SINGLENESS

"But as many as received him, to them gave he power to become the sons of God, even to them that believe on his name" — John 1:12

THE SINGLE LIFE

GETTING TO KNOW THE REAL YOU

Take time to develop and to learn about yourself before you enter in a relationship. If you don't, you'll lean on the other person for your identity. You need to be all right with yourself before you enter any relationship, so you know exactly who God created you to become. In doing so, you'll avoid becoming co-dependent on that relationship. Instead, be the strong man or woman of God that you're predestined to be.

You must love yourself enough to know that being in a relationship doesn't make you somebody great! Only Christ can do that for you. You are already God's beloved, and He wants nothing more but for you to walk in joy, not just during this season, but during all seasons of your life.

As Christians, our goal is to improve through Christ. We should consider every struggle a chance to trust in the Lord and to overcome every obstacle. Once we accept that challenge, the Lord uses it to mold us into that better person He wants us to be. Think of some flaws that have become habits for you.

Matthew 14 says that Peter walked across the waves on the Sea of Galilee because his eyes were on Jesus. But as soon as he took his eyes off Jesus and put them on his surroundings, he began to sink. When we stay focused on Jesus, we too can walk across the tops of the waves of life, undamaged by the fear of experiencing what we see happening to others.

You may feel lonely and unfulfilled at times, no matter which stage of life you're in. But don't meditate on that thought; go on a journey instead. Do something you love to do. If you fill your time with meaningful activities, you'll find you are beginning to develop the person the Lord has called you to be. Regardless of how challenging life becomes, do not allow yourself to feel sorry about the path your life has taken thus far.

If you are single, learn the importance of taking care of yourself before you date or marry. Feel okay doing activities that make you happy and help you improve personally. Get a massage, take a hot bath, join an exercise class, go for a walk, travel, or shop. Whatever you do that is healthy for you, include that activity in your life.

SETTING GOALS AND OBJECTIVES

Begin to gauge how long it may take to fulfill some of the dreams you have set in your heart for improving your relationship with the Lord. If you don't set a date to get started with your plan, it may take you a lot longer than you think to accomplish that plan.

First, write three goals and some objectives on a piece of paper, or type them into your computer, phone, or tablet. That way, you'll begin to visibly see your dreams come true.

Next, set a timeline to complete those goals and begin to mark them on your calendar. The dates remind you of what you can do each day to fulfill something small on your list.

When goals involve others, set up meetings with these individuals and assign yourself daily tasks related to your self-improvement goals that you'll complete between meetings. These bite-sized actions help keep you motivated and on task to help you fine tune the gifts God has given you and achieve your long- term dreams.

When you begin to fulfill your goals, reward yourself in small ways. Rewards are important motivators for the future and serve as reminders of what God has accomplished in your life.

Review them often as you walk out your journey and look back on these personal milestones. It's amazing to see a lifelong dream that God has given you come true right before your eyes.

Don't be too hard on yourself. Nobody is perfect and the Lord knows all of us are works in progress. But take time to sit and think on the things you want to see changed. Focus on the areas where God is showing you there needs to be improvement. That needed change begins to manifest when we focus our eyes on Jesus and what He wants us to do. Seeing our lives through His eyes and viewing His plan for us changes our perspective.

EXPLORING YOUR GIFTS AND TALENTS

Can you imagine getting paid to do what you love? People who use their God-given talents and abilities in their work generally say they don't feel as if they've worked a day in their lives. God created everyone with unique gifts and talents. It's such a reassuring and edifying feeling to be living your authentic self.

Matthew 25:15-18 says:

> And unto one he gave five talents, to another two, and to another one; to every man according to his several abilities; and straightway took his journey. Then he that had received the five talents went and traded with the same, and made them other five talents. And likewise, he that had received two, he also gained other two. But he that had received one went and digged in the earth, and hid his lord's money.

This is an excellent example of God reminding us to be faithful stewards of every gift and talent

He has given us. To further develop these gifts, we must dedicate time to using them instead of burying them where no one can see them. God will bless you when you decide to develop them and commit time to learning all you can about them. This will set you up to learn more about who you are and where you are going in life.

Getting to know your gifts and talents can be a challenging and exciting process. The first step is to cultivate your relationship with the Lord, Jesus Christ. God said to Jeremiah in 1:5,

"Before I formed thee in the belly I knew thee; and before thou camest forth out of the womb I sanctified thee, and I ordained thee a prophet unto the nations."

God created you, so He knows more about you than you know about yourself. Learning about Him, therefore, is the true roadmap to learning all there is to know about your purpose. Taking

this time to pursue your personal relationship with your Heavenly Father, through daily
reading of your Bible and seeking God through
your personal devotional and prayer time, will
help you find your true gifts and talents.

DISCOVERING YOUR LIKES
AND DISLIKES

It's so important to discover your likes and
dislikes in your spiritual life, social life, work,
family, school, and so on. Begin by thinking
back to your childhood to reflect on what you
liked and disliked; these reflections can be true
representations of your genuine self.

We're not born from our mothers' wombs
knowing who we are and what we want. But as
we journey through life, we discover clues of
who God calls us to become. With some extra
effort on our parts, God reveals these special
clues to us daily, and this journey of discovery

with Him is such a delight. The extra focus on His will for us makes our journeys brighter.

Everyone, including your mother, may want to give you advice about what you should like and dislike, but these are choices only you can make. Do what you enjoy, not what your friends or family want you to do, if their choices don't fit your life.

What you don't want is to live the life your boy-friend or girlfriend wants for you. You will only grow to resent yourself and the person you are dating if you are not being your genuine self. If you persist in this kind of relationship, you'll leave angry and frustrated and begin to blame other people for your unhappiness.

You want the confidence that comes from knowing who you are inside before you begin to plan your future with someone else. So, thoroughly examine your spiritual walk, job, career, social life, school, geography, family, and friends before you commit to another person.

LIVING THE SINGLE LIFE

Living the single life is such a blessing even though it gets a bad rap in this day and time. Part of the problem is that marketing campaigns set you up with unreasonable expectations for what your life should be and when. This outlook can make you believe you're not complete until you get married.

Count your journey as a blessing and not a curse. If you believe God has called you to remain single for a more dedicated life or missions work, then that's exactly what you should do. If you believe you're called to marriage, but you're still single, don't become impatient. Allow the fruit of patience to complete its work in your life and enjoy the peace while you have it.

Choosing to receive support to help in each stage of singleness can make the biggest difference in the world. Allow your accountability partner to mentor or disciple you during moments of frustration and pain. The knowledge you gain by overcoming one hardship prepares you to face your next battle. Trials and tribulations can show you where you really are instead of where you think you might be in your walk with God.

Decide to enjoy each season, instead of murmuring, complaining, or being too eager to jump to the next stage. As you experience unexpected challenges, you may feel as if there is a huge gap between where you are and where you believe God wants you to be. Whether you're single or married, Romans 8:28 says, "And we know that all things work together for good to them that love God, to them who are the called according to his purpose."

GETTING TO KNOW THE LORD

As a Christian, one of the most important decisions you'll ever make is accepting Jesus Christ as your personal Lord and Savior. This essential step will not only fulfill the void that lies deep within your heart, but it is a major clue in trying to get to know who you are. It's hard to get to know the real you without accepting and having a relationship with the Lord Jesus Christ.

We all face trials and tribulations. So, it's important for us to know that the Lord Jesus Christ uses the hardships in our lives to strengthen us. As you work through seasons of difficulty, remind yourself of who God has created you to be. Decide even before you encounter a situation to respond with love and kindness rather than frustration and anger.

Choose to face each circumstance with a grateful heart. Speak words that the trial will have its perfect work in your life. You can have what you say. As you do, God will send you a peace that comes from knowing He has your back. King David did this often as he prepared for battle.

Corinthians 12:9-10 says,

> "And he said unto me, My grace is sufficient for thee: for my strength is made perfect in weakness. Most gladly therefore will I rather glory in my infirmities, that the power of Christ may rest upon me. Therefore I take pleasure in infirmities, in reproaches, in necessities, in persecutions, in distresses for Christ's sake: for when I am weak, then am I strong."

God never leaves or abandons you, no matter what is going on in your life. A season of having nowhere to turn except the Lord can be a great barometer to reveal where you stand in God and how important He is to you. As you begin each new phase of your life, the knowledge you gain in these seasons will be invaluable.

ARE YOU READY FOR A RELATIONSHIP?

One telltale sign that says you're ready to say "yes" to a relationship is when you become content with being a single man or woman. So, enjoy your preparation time, even though you desire marriage. Wait patiently on the Lord, and He will send you the right man or woman.

You will attract an individual just like you, so work on eliminating as many weaknesses as you can so you can be complete (not perfect) before your spouse comes along. If you're not content with the person you are today, dating or marrying the right person will not fulfill that empty void.

God did not create that person to eliminate your loneliness and make you happy. Only God can satisfy that yearning for something deeper inside you. You must be happy alone before you can truly be happy with a life partner.

Write down five clues that show you're emotionally ready for a relationship. Then make a list of five struggles that show you aren't ready. Next, list five reasons that indicate this is your season to date.

Ask yourself the following questions:

1. Do I have trust issues?
2. Do I still have pain in my heart from a past relationship?
3. Do I carry baggage from my younger life into this relationship?
4. Do I fear the "what if's"?

If you answered "yes" to any of these questions, allow yourself to be vulnerable and seek professional advice if necessary, particularly if you need emotional healing. Don't feel embarrassed about any areas of your life that need help or accountability.

It is not a character flaw to have weaknesses; in fact, they are blessings that allow God to help you develop the fruits of His Spirit in you. Your circumstances can help you bear fruit and set you up for success, not failure.

TAKE A MOMENT AND ANSWER THESE QUESTIONS.

SINGLE LIFE GETTING TO KNOW THE REAL YOU

List 3 random facts about yourself.

1.

2.

3.

SETTING GOALS & OBJECTIVES

List 3 goals for your life, and 3 objectives, or ways to accomplish those goals.

Goals

1.

2.

3.

Objectives

1.

2.

3.

EXPLORING YOUR GIFTS AND TALENTS

List 3 of your gifts and talents.

1.

2.

3.

DISCOVERING YOUR LIKES AND DISLIKES

List 3 things you like and 3 things you dislike.

Likes

1.

2.

3.

Dislikes

1.

2.

3.

LIVING THE SINGLE LIFE
List two benefits of living the single life.

1.   ;
2.

GETTING TO KNOW THE REAL YOU
List 3 of your strengths.

1.

2.

3.

List 3 of your weaknesses.

1.

2.

3.

ARE YOU READY FOR A RELATIONSHIP?
Write down 3 signs that show a person is ready to be in a relationship.

1.

2.

3.

DATING

"Can two walk together, except they be agreed?" Amos 3:3

DIFFERENT WAYS TO COMMUNICATE

Thanks to the Internet and social media, there are more ways to communicate than ever before: talking and texting on the phone, Skyping, emailing, or chatting on Facebook, just to name a few. "Couples" are using all these ways to learn if they share similar goals and interests before they go out on their first dates.

While you're on your first date, ask the other person relevant questions about his or her upbringing without making the person feel "interviewed." Asking and answering questions openly allows both of you to genuinely get to know one another through a meaningful discussion of your lives and values up to this point.

Because you are dating with the intent to find that special someone, ask the other person about his or her faith during your discussion, especially since 2 Corinthians 6:14 warns us not to marry someone who is not a Christian: "Be ye not unequally yoked together with unbelievers: for what fellowship hath righteousness with unrighteousness? and what communion hath light with darkness?"

THE FOLLOWING ARE SOME POTENTIAL QUESTIONS TO WORK INTO YOUR DATE AS CASUALLY AS POSSIBLE:

- How did you come to know Jesus as your Savior?
- How long have you attended church?
- Tell me about your childhood.
- Have you ever been married?
- Are your parents married?
- Do you have any children?
- What are your hobbies?
- Where do you work?

HANGING OUT GROUP STYLE

Group dating is a fun and safe way to discover whether you and your potential mate have the personality traits you are seeking in one another. So much happens in this world that it is almost a must to include this step in your process.

Dating in a group of friends doesn't show 100 percent of the individual, but it allows friends of both dating partners to give their opinions about your date and the two of you together.

Each of you should bring at least two people who know you well to the group date for input. These can be couples or singles. Being among friends takes the pressure off those tough moments of silence and gives you a more relaxed atmosphere.

A singles group in a Christian environment also provides an excellent environment for group dating. Please practice good safety tips. If you ever feel unsafe, let an employee or someone know that you're in danger.

1. Always let someone know where and who you will be with you.
2. Have your cellphone charged in case of an emergency.
3. Meet in a public place.
4. Always pay attention to your surroundings on your way to meet the individual.
5. Never let your date know your residence or place of work .

THE HONEYMOON STAGE

The honeymoon stage is the beginning of a relationship when people show their best to each other. Human nature causes us to pull out all the stops to impress our potential mates in the early stages of a relationship.

We find it so easy to show them our strengths and to try to sell them on how perfect we are in that moment. Truthfully, everyone knows there's no such thing as a perfect person, but we still try to display the image of perfection to those we're interested in romantically.

Exploring each other's distinct personalities involves learning the desirable and undesirable traits that exist inside your hearts. Allowing your date to see those sides you may not be as willing to show helps develop trust. Even if your date doesn't show his or her character flaws right off the bat, again, none of us are perfect.

Pay close attention to your inner being, your natural, God given intuition that alerts you to "red flags," such as character flaws, criminal records, a hidden divorce, or even that your dating partner isn't dating to marry. Unfortunately, you may even discover the person you're going out with is already married!

Bottom line: If something doesn't seem right, trust your instincts. We live in a society that preys on women and men for different reasons, so your instincts can be blessings in disguise. I don't know how many men and women I've counseled who have said they wish they would have trusted that inner voice or feeling telling them something wasn't right. It was too good to be true.

DOES THIS PERSON HAVE A HEART FOR YOU?

As you get to know your dating (and potential marriage) partner, you can determine if he or she has a heart for you by looking at his or her actions:

- When the two of you are together, what kind of behavior does he/she display? Are they positive or negative?

- If negative, how consistent is he or she with those traits? Is the person willing to change?
- Can he/she admit when he/she is wrong? How does he/she apologize?
- How long do your fights last? Are you able to talk about the fight after the dust has cleared?
- Does he/she use sarcasm to put you down in front of others? When he/she puts you down, is it in a joking style?
- Does he/she stand up for you when someone else is putting you down? Is he/she protective of you?
- Does he/she want to break up every time he's/she's angry with you?

Does your boyfriend and girlfriend have a heart for you? If you find that your boyfriend/girlfriend doesn't have a heart for you, please consider getting wise counsel so you have strength to get out of that relationship.

WHEN YOU THINK THIS IS "THE ONE"
Even though today's secular society often thinks it absurd to date with the goal of marriage, as a Christian, while dating someone, you must clearly show that individual you desire a serious courtship.

When you are introducing someone into your world, never be deceitful about your intentions. Communicate openly. Both of you must make sure you want the same thing. Entering a relationship with trust and honesty is a cornerstone for a strong marriage.

Always show your cards; never hide anything. God will richly bless you for it. Once you're on the same page, discuss what you both think is a reasonable amount of time to date before becoming engaged. Always be open and flexible if either of you desire to date for a longer time than the other before becoming engaged.

Proverb 11:3 says,

> "The integrity of the upright shall
> guide them: but the perverseness of
> transgressors shall destroy them."

DATING FOR A GOOD LENGTH OF TIME

I challenge you to date at least two years before saying "I do" so you can really get to know each other. At this point, you might be saying, "My parents dated for three months, and they've been happily married for twenty-five years!"

That may be so, but dating someone for less than two years is a major risk, as it is often not enough time for each to discover the other's virtues and flaws. Court each other long enough to see your potential mate's weaknesses and how he/she behaves when faced with challenges.

Just because someone is a good businesswoman doesn't mean she would be a good wife. Some people find it hard to juggle a relationship and a job, while others say the "balancing act" makes them better in each role.

At some point when you are alone, consider the following questions to help you decide whether the person you're dating is the person you want to spend the rest of your life with:

- Do his/her characteristics fit your most important characteristics in a mate?
- Do his/her actions contradict what he/she says?
- Is he/she following the Lord in his/her interactions with others when the two of you are together?
- Does he/she treat you well when you are in private or public?

TAKE A MOMENT AND ANSWER THESE QUESTIONS.

DATING DIFFERENT WAYS TO COMMUNICATE

List 3 different ways a potential couple can communicate before going on a date.

1.

2.

3.

HANGING OUT GROUP STYLE

List 3 potential activities for a group date.

1.

2.

3.

THE HONEYMOON STAGE
List 3 signs that indicate a couple is in the honeymoon stage.

1.

2.

3.

DOES THIS PERSON HAVE A
HEART FOR YOU?
List 3 signs that state he/she has a heart for you.

1.

2.

3.

WHEN YOU THINK THIS IS THE ONE

List 3 reasons why you think the person you are dating is "the one."

1.

2.

3.

DATING FOR A GOOD LENGTH OF TIME
List 3 reasons why it is important to date for at least two years.

1.

2.

3.

PRE-MARITAL LIFE

"It is not good that the man should be alone"
Genesis 2:18

BECOMING ENGAGED

Once you believe the dating season has helped you see what you want in a marriage, and you have found a special connection with someone who could potentially be "the one," preparing for engagement is an exciting time in your life.

Get opinions from your accountability team about your potential plan of engagement. Allow them to speak into your life with any concerns before a final decision is made. Their feedback may just challenge you to consider a few things you may have overlooked, a bit more.

Use your accountability partners to examine your core beliefs about your potential mate:

- Can this person be counted on to follow through with what he/she says?
- Can he/she trust you to keep your word?

- Has your relationship improved over the last six months to a year?
- Has each of you asked God whether you are the right person for each other?

It's normal and healthy to meet someone that is flawed because all of us are. Everyone comes into a relationship with baggage; no one's perfect. Your goal should be to communicate with the person to see if the two of you are like-minded. This will help if the two of you get married one day because conflicts arise in every marriage. You can avoid major issues early on by agreeing to take any conflicts to the Lord.

It's critical to date someone long enough to see him or her go through hardships, so you can discover his or her weaknesses. Infidelity, abuse, and addictions can become deal-breakers in a relationship. Finding out about any hidden struggles beforehand avoids surprises on your wedding day or in your marriage.

If, however, you choose to date someone who has an addiction, and that person is seeking help and wants to change, enter the courtship with forgiveness and a supportive mindset. Keep in mind, however, there are no guarantees change will be successful, and addiction can be a life-long struggle. Even if in the end you decide to be friends instead of boyfriend and girlfriend, this friendship will be lifelong.

HOW DO YOU PREPARE FOR MARRIED LIFE?

Once you're engaged, talk to a marriage counselor before the wedding plans are made. Getting advice from a counselor provides neutral ground for developing communication skills you will need for your future life as a married couple.

This can help prevent distresses that require counseling after marriage. It also provides support and accountability to both of you as you learn to communicate with each other more effectively.

Consider the following for a successful marriage.

1. Get joint counseling
2. Have an accountability couple mentor you
3. Guard your heart and mind
4. Live within your financial means

Learn to laugh more and enjoy your engagement process. All work and no play can make life unbearable, so plan your fun to laugh and enjoy your journey. God has given us so much to be thankful for in our everyday lives. We often take these blessings for granted until our journey brings us to a place where we are confronted with what we don't have in life that we still want.

MAKE A LIST OF EXPECTATIONS

Set goals in your relationship so you can reach your God-given dreams. Goals help set the direction for the dreams God has given you as you determine the steps necessary to achieve them. Each of you (separately) should write where you want to see yourselves in the next one to five years and switch papers to see what the other wrote.

If you struggle with this question, think of other marriages you admire. Thinking about what you admire most in them will give you some ideas of what you would like to achieve as a couple. Or, think of areas where you are currently facing challenges and write what you want to eliminate in the future.

Write your ideas together, sharing thoughts and objectives with each other. This is extremely healthy in providing a significant path for your family to follow. Since each of your desires will be highlighted from the very start, this exercise can help draw you closer as you see those desires being fulfilled.

So instead of becoming stagnant and growing apart, you will naturally want to hold each other accountable for your goals and objectives so you achieve the quality lifestyle you are seeking as a couple.

MAKE A LIST OF DEAL-BREAKERS

Make a list of items that would cause you to walk away from your relationship if the other party decided to engage in them. This may be a tough and scary step but should be considered mandatory.

Are you involved in a relationship where some of these demeaning offenses have occurred? Here are a few examples to include in your list of deal-breakers. Abuse (physical, sexual, or verbal); having an affair; or being controlling or jealous.

Here are questions to consider.

- Does he/she blame everybody except himself/herself for problems that arise?
- Does he/she isolate you?
- How does he/she act when upset?
- Is there any yelling or name calling? Or are you able to discuss issues in a civilized manner?
- Is there any infidelity, abuse, gambling, anger, addictions, etc., between you two?
- Does he/she look at porn?
- Is he/she secretly talking, texting, emailing, going to coffee, and going out with another man or women?

If you find yourself in this kind of relationship, please get help right away!

TACKLE THE TOUGH ISSUES

Openly and honestly discuss your earliest moments of pain and hardship that still trigger you today, and let God reveal to you where He wants to bring healing and restoration. It's never too late to grow beyond your past mistakes.

It's easy to see the flaws of others without looking at ourselves. It's important to address your own weaknesses so you can enter marriage as a blessing rather than a curse to your spouse. Never enter marriage thinking, What about me?

All of us need to make changes in our behaviors as we live our lives, so there is no time like now. Allow God to convict you and show you where you need to change. God's purpose is for you to grow in His grace and in His knowledge.

We can either surrender to His mighty hand while He's working with us or reject it. No matter what, God has a way of producing in us what He needs us to change. It's easier to do it when it first comes up instead of hanging onto it until the Lord forces our hands. So be open to the Lord Jesus Christ, and let His peace and mercy rule in your life.

Build on the wonderful knowledge you've learned about each other thus far. Talk through your answers to the following questions so you can get to know each other in a more intense way.

All the issues and questions identified up to this point would be discussed further during pre-marital counseling.

ENGAGEMENT

Becoming engaged will be one of the most memorable days in your life. It is saying yes to someone who you believe is the one you'll spend your life

Have you two discussed any weaknesses in your relationship that you are determined not to carry into your marriage? If so, what are those boundaries, and are you both living out those boundaries now? Take some time to discuss healthy boundaries for your marriage to come?

Take a minute and answer the following questions.

- Are there any red flags in your relationship? Is so, list and discuss them.
- Will you be a two-career household, or will one be responsible for the duties at home instead of working outside the home?
- Who did the chores in each of your households when you two were young?
- Have you discussed who will do the household chores when you're married?
- What godly fruit or characteristics does your fiancé (or fiancée) display? What are they?

- Have you two been through any tough trials while dating? If so, what happened and how did you both experience it?
- Are you and your fiancé (or fiancée) able to accept and offer criticism? If no, why not?
- What does it mean to have marriage as a covenant and how do we uphold our positions as husband and wife?

YOUR LOVE LANGUAGES

Every individual was born with a love tank.

In his book *The Five Love Languages*, Gary Chapman discusses five primary ways people express love: Touch, Words of Affirmation, Quality Time, Gifts, and Acts Service.

Understanding the ways, the two of you express love toward one another is key for both of you to know how you prefer to receive or express love.

I would gift it to anyone who's in a relationship! It is such a wonderful example of how we should love the other person exactly how God designed them. Take a minute and discuss what are your top two love languages

- Discuss the five love languages
- How do you plan to show love to your spouse?
- What are the top two love languages you can't live without? Provide examples.
- How are you implementing your love to one another?

ACCOUNTABILITY

Accountability is allowing an individual, couple or group to mentor, coach, confront, and teach you skills that will make your life better. These need to be Christians who live by their faith, are trustworthy, and won't judge you because of any trials you may be facing.

These folks will always see you as though you weren't facing any struggle. Your panel also needs to be objective, so they can't be people who idolize you, your spiritual walk, or your career.

Allow those you selected to speak openly and objectively, without hesitation, and without the fear that your friendship might end abruptly because they spoke truth to you. They need to be able to give objective opinions when you need clarity. And you need opportunity to ask for their perspectives, no matter how you feel about what they might say.

As they come to know your story--the good, the bad, and the ugly--they will urge you to do the work needed to develop yourself and take you to the next level in your spiritual walk.

Let this accountability create hope, support, and encouragement in and through you. 2 Timothy

3:16 says, "All Scripture is God-breathed and is useful for teaching, rebuking, correcting and training in righteousness."

BOUNDARIES

A boundary in a relationship is letting your yes be yes and your no be no. It's refusing to allow others control or dictate what is good and healthy for your own life. It's setting guidelines and rules, and creating a barrier for others to respect your view.

"Two are better than one; because they have a good reward for their labor. For if they fall, the one will lift his fellow: but woe to him that is alone when he falleth; for he hath not another to help him up." — Ecclesiastes 4:9-10

- Are there issues or habits either of you have noticed since you have been dating or engaged that you don't want to bring to your marriage? If so, please list and discuss.

- What are you not willing to put up with in this relationship?
- How do you enable bad behavior?

FINANCES

Take some time to get hard core facts about each other's financial situation. Find out each other's debt and FICA score.

This step must be done because finances are among the leading causes of stress in a marriage. When you marry that individual, their past financial debt will affect you. Take a minute and answer these questions.

- Do you have debt?
- What is your FICA score?
- Have you ever had to file for bankruptcy?
- Do you both have money in savings? If so, how much?

- Do you have enough money together for a down payment on a house?
- Are you prepared for emergencies?
- Who will handle the money? Will the two have a will?
- Will you both work?
- Who will pay for your insurance packages? (These include investments, life insurance, health insurance, vision insurance, and dental insurance.)
- Who will handle bank accounts?

CHORES

When you get married and move in with one another, you will have to share the load of work responsibilities, inside and outside. So, setting up a shared list of chores before marriage can assure you a lot more peace after you say, "I do."

Start by making a list of all the chores that you need to be done around the house. Try to focus on what chores would make sense for each other's schedule.

Although these questions can be annoying, you should set them up and discuss to hear each other's opinions on what works for one another. You would be surprised how easy an argument begins between the two of you when it comes to who does what chores and when.

Answer the following questions.

INDOOR WORK

- Who will cook each week (are you going to rotate)?
- Who will clean the dishes after one-person cooks?
- Who will take out the garbage?
- Who will wash the clothes?
- Who will vacuum?
- Who will dust?
- Who will make the bed?

OUTDOOR WORK

- Who will cut the yard?
- Who will take care of the gardening?
- Who will take out the garbage?
- Who will shovel snow in the winter?

TRY SETTING A CALENDAR THAT LOOKS SOMETHING LIKE THIS:

TASK	MONDAY	TUESDAY	WEDNESDAY	THURSDAY	FRIDAY
KITCHEN					
COOKING					
DISHES					
LAUNDRY					

DO WE AGREE?

You can end up going to counseling arguing and disclosing each other's weaknesses. It's relatively common to find out information about each other that you were unaware of before.

You may have found out, for example, that your fiancé (or fiancée) has more debt than you originally knew.

There are times where people cancel wedding dates because of the other person saying, "We need six more months to pay off that debt."

Don't go into this session without being honest with one another, because you fear the other person might get angry with you or hold it over your head. You must start by being open about subjects that concern or worry you. You can't hold back; you must start speaking what's on your heart.

At the end of your premarital counseling sessions, what would you do if the counselor recommended you wait another year before getting married? Would you take his or her advice?

Corinthians 13:11 says,

> "When I was a child, I spake as
> a child, I understood as a child,
> I thought as a child: but when I

became a man, I put away childish things."

Each of us goes through a time in our lives where we begin to grow up and abandon immature behavior, exchanging it for the fruits of the Spirit. Galatians 5:22-23 says, "But the fruit of the Spirit is love, joy, peace, longsuffering, gentleness, goodness, faith, Meekness, temperance: against such there is no law." Devoting your time and your attention to studying God's Word, attending a Bible study, and praying are the keys to developing the fruits of the Spirit. These keys help you dig deeper in God's Word and cultivate your relationship with Him.

TAKE A MOMENT AND ANSWER THESE QUESTIONS

PRE-MARITAL LIFE

List 3 signs that the time is right to become engaged.

1.

2.

3.

HOW DO YOU PREPARE FOR MARRIED LIFE?

List 3 ways to prepare for married life.

1.

2.

3.

MAKE A LIST OF EXPECTATIONS

List 3 expectations you have for married life.

1. .

2.

3.

MAKE A LIST OF DEAL BREAKERS

List 3 deal-breakers that would potentially destroy your engagement or marriage.

1.

2.

3.

TACKLE THE TOUGH ISSUES

List 3 guidelines you have for tackling tough issues in your relationship.

1.

2.

3.

ENGAGEMENT
List 3 reasons why you are engaged.

1.

2.

YOUR LOVE LANGUAGES
List your top two love languages.

1.

2.

ACCOUNTABILITY
List 1 or 2 couples who can hold you accountable.

1.

2.

BOUNDARIES

List 3 boundaries you have set or plan to set in your relationship.

1.

2.

3.

FINANCES

Find out each other's FICA score. List any debt you have.

1.

2.

3.

CHORES

Make a list of your indoor responsibilities.

1.

2.

OUTDOOR WORK
Make a list of your outdoor responsibilities.

1.

2.

DO WE AGREE?
List 3 tell-tale signs that you two agree on an issue.

1.

2.

3.

MARRIAGE FOUNDATION

"Two are better than one; because they have a good reward for their labor. For if they fall, the one will   lift his fellow: but woe to him that is alone when he falleth; for he hath not another to help him up. Again, if two lie together, then they have heat: but how can one be warm alone? And if one prevails against him, two shall withstand him; and a threefold cord is not quickly broken."

Ecclesiastes 4:9-12

SETTING PROTOCOLS FOR THE FUTURE

Protocols are simply boundaries for what you desire and want from each other. This is divorce-proofing your marriage before it starts.

It's always important to know what you will put up with and what you won't put up with before you walk down the aisle. Healthy boundaries define expectations and show respect for each other. So, voice your wishes and hopes to your spouse before you marry.

Marriage is about two imperfect people coming together under one roof, which means every marriage will have troubles. The good news is that you have come together with the Lord, who can perfect the two of you, unite you, and sanctify your marriage (which means make it holy).

When you come together in unity with God, you come together with a desire to birth goals into reality. The Lord promises in Mark 11:23-24 that whatsoever we ask in faith He will give us. Wherever two or more of us are gathered in His name, He is there with us.

We are all on a journey to work hard and grow in God's grace in His knowledge. Galatians 5:22-23 says the fruits of the Spirit are "love, joy, peace, longsuffering, gentleness, goodness, faith, meekness, temperance: against such there is no law." These fruits are needed as much or more in a marriage as in any other relationship.

BEGIN TO WALK OUT PROTOCOLS

Make a list of topics you struggle with and how you would tell each other what you want in your marriage. Examples might include ways to handle the in-laws or ways to handle the opposite sex. List ways you hope the other person will behave and how you will handle when your ideals are not met.

Giving yourselves a way to communicate your differences will take some stress out of the relationship if you know in advance what it is that you do that bothers the other person. To receive grace, you must give grace.

Discuss the areas in each other's lives that could be changed. When you fail, try again. Ask Christ to help you. Reconcile your relationship with Him if you haven't already done so. And don't give up on each other because you don't get it right the first few times. Many of us have lived the way we have for a long time. Our past is what makes us unique. Be willing to forgive before the end of the day. The Word of God states: Don't let the sun go down on your anger.

Find out any hardships your potential spouse faced growing up. Outline the triggers for anger and temptation. Are you both willing to seek assistance with those concerns in your lives that were previously "unmarked territory"?

Even after you're married, you still might see some red flags that indicate a problem in the relationship. Address them with your spouse, in counseling if necessary. Some behaviors may include, but aren't limited to hiding his/ her cell phone, leaving the house without saying where he/she is going, and appearing differently at home than in public.

AGAPE LOVE

Ephesians 5:1-2 says "Be ye therefore followers of God, as dear children; And walk in love, as Christ also hath loved us, and hath given himself for us an offering and a sacrifice to God for a sweet-smelling savior."

- Love is an action word.
- Love is self-sacrificing. You will never feel like loving someone who wrongs you.
- So just because you feel uncomfortable loving anyway and forgiving the person when he/she wrongs you, that

doesn't mean you have hidden hostility toward him/her.

- Love is not about trying. If you try or say you can't, the reality is you won't!

The Bible talks about how easy it is to love someone who loves you, but it's harder to love someone when everything is going haywire. During those moments, we must remain consistent toward our spouses in our household routines and behaviors, regardless of how we feel. A good marriage requires both partners to walk in unconditional love even when they don't feel as if they deserve it.

You don't stop cleaning your home or cooking for each other just because you don't feel like it. You are married. Having this consistency in your life will help you get through rough patches.

Choose to be mature instead of giving in to your flesh or emotions. Deciding to be consistent in your home routine will bring peace to you and your spouse. We are called to love and serve each other.

LOVE DEFINED

As believers, our love walk means more to God than anything in this world. In marriage, you will have ups and downs, but it's important that you choose to love over sin. Let your fruits of the Spirit reign in your life, regardless of your present circumstances.

Love is a spiritual warfare strategy, and love in action will destroy anything demonic that comes your way. Love is also a sign of maturity, especially when you choose to love one another through any hardship.

1 Corinthians 13:4-8 says about love:

> Charity suffereth long, and is kind; charity envieth not; charity

vaunteth not itself, is not puffed up, Doth not behave itself unseemly, seeketh not her own, is not easily provoked, thinketh no evil; Rejoiceth not in iniquity, but rejoiceth in the truth; Beareth all things, believeth all things, hopeth all things, endureth all things. Charity never faileth: but whether there be prophecies, they shall fail; whether there be tongues, they shall cease; whether there be knowledge, it shall vanish away.

LOVE IS PATIENT

The Lord uses marriage to increase the fruits of the Spirit in us. God calls us to be patient with one another. Doing something for your spouse instead of doing something for yourself will leave you feeling blessed. The Bible says it's better to give than to receive. Always have a heart to serve and give instead of always assuming your spouse will serve you.

If your heart is, "I can't wait to marry so I can have someone take care of me," you are being unrealistic. You can't begin a successful marriage that way.

Also, pick and choose your battles. If your spouse irritates you, be willing to turn the other cheek. Be a helpmate, not a scorekeeper. Don't remind your spouse how many times you did a job or how many times she made a certain comment, and so on.

Love protects. Don't vent to everyone about how horrible your spouse is. Protect your spouse and get your accountability partners to help with that.

Love suffers long. Don't say you want a divorce every time something happens that doesn't meet your approval.

Always love and forgive. If you say you are a believer, you are called by God to let yesterday go, so don't carry it on for weeks to come.

CREATING DISCIPLINE IN YOUR MARRIAGE

Nothing replaces hard work. If you don't put in the work needed to fulfill your God-given dreams in marriage, you will not receive the results you often fantasize about. Your marriage may seem stressful at times, but I promise the results of hard work are much greater than you can imagine.

One key to a happy marriage is to stop offending your spouse with the same behaviors over and over. What you think is controlling, your wife may see as "getting things in order." If for example, she walks into the room and closes the blinds without asking permission, your perspective as the husband might be, "There she goes again, trying to control whether I can look out the window."

It doesn't matter whether you call it controlling or the wife calls it "getting things in order." When the behavior offends your spouse, CHANGE IT! STOP DOING IT!

WHAT IF YOUR SPOUSE IS STRUGGLING?

If your spouse is struggling in the marriage, get some help. If he/she refuses the help, get counseling for yourself so you have some encouragement. Then you will be less tempted to leave because of your emotions. Always create a protocol for getting help if this same issue goes on for months.

Ask yourself these questions:

1. How do you work out your arguments?
2. How long does it take?
3. How long do you hold a grudge?
4. What are the top two trials you've been through as an individual and as a couple?
5. Explain how you worked them out.
6. Does your spouse hold onto behaviors such as not forgiving, resentment, and bitterness?
7. Discuss these items in counseling so your and your spouse's weaknesses can be addressed.

Ephesians 4:31-32 tells us we can strengthen our lives by putting away all bitterness, wrath, anger, lying, backbiting, and unforgiveness. In their place, Ephesians 5:22-23 says we can put on love, joy, peace, longsuffering, gentleness, goodness, faith, meekness, and temperance. Seek to change by taking the time to discover the root cause of these sinful behaviors that have become patterns. Attend a Bible study, or seek the help of a life coach or a counselor to help you develop the areas where you are lacking. That's how you will gain strength and develop confidence to do what God has called you to do. Make a decision work on your marriage and invest the time and money that's necessary to improve things.

MARRIAGE FOUNDATION

SETTING PROTOCOLS FOR THE FUTURE

BEGIN TO WALK OUT PROTOCOLS

List 3 protocols you are using in your marriage.

1.

2.

3.

AGAPE LOVE

List 3 sacrifices you have made for each other.

1.

2.

3.

LOVE DEFINED

We are called to love and serve each other.
List 3 ways you have served each other in love.

1.

2.

3.

LOVE IS PATIENT LIST

3 ways you have walked in patience with one another.

1.

2.

3.

CREATING DISCIPLINE IN YOUR MARRIAGE

List 3 ways you intend to create healthy discipline in your marriage.

1.

2.

3.

WHAT IF YOUR SPOUSE IS STRUGGLING?

List 3 people you can reach out to for help if your spouse is struggling.

1.

2.

3.

IN CONCLUSION

It's important to remember to enjoy the first stage of your life – being single – to the fullest before you decide to date someone. Use this time to learn and know exactly who you are, what you want from life, and what you want in a mate. That way potential mates will more closely resemble your ideal mate.

Go on group dates with other friends so other couples can give you feedback about how your potential mate interacts with others before you become emotionally involved with him/her. This will help you get to know the individual so you can make a healthy decision whether to date him/her.

Dating someone for a couple of years, with the intention of getting to know one another well, allows the "honeymoon" phase of trying to impress each other to fade. When you date the person long enough to see the good, the bad, and the ugly in him/her, you begin to see the whole person. Everyone has strengths and weaknesses, but some weaknesses can dissolve a relationship.

After proposing to this special someone (or after your special someone proposes to you) in the third stage, use the engagement period to know your fiancé (or fiancée) even better before you say, "I do." Begin to prepare for marriage by creating a great biblical foundation. Get solid, biblical, premarital counseling from a Bible-based counselor or from taking a Bible premarital class.

When you're married (fourth stage), always maintain the following order in your marriage: Christ first, your relationship second, and children third. Always be open to touch base with a biblical counselor when you need help. Be willing to have recurring date nights and go on yearly trips. Never stop investing in time together and in dating one another. These tips will keep your friendship alive as time progresses.

Life is such a gift! It can be an exciting yet challenging journey. The success of it depends on your attitude; decide with open arms and a grateful heart to follow your purpose and plan. 1 Corinthians 2:9 says, "But as it is written, Eye hath not seen, nor ear heard, neither have entered into the heart of man, the things which God hath prepared for them that love him." On this trip, get to know the real you while allowing God to mold you.

BIBLIOGRAPHY

Chapman, Gary D. *The 5 Love Languages.*
(Chicago: Northfield, 2015).

The Bible. *Authorized King James Version.*
(Thomas Nelson, 1976).

CPSIA information can be obtained
at www.ICGtesting.com
Printed in the USA
BVOW08s0937290118
506601BV00001B/15/P